a gift to:

from:

date:

Published in Nashville, Tennessee, by Thomas Nelson, Inc.

Unless otherwise indicated, Scripture quotations are taken from *The Holy Bible, New
Century Version*, copyright © 1987, 1988, 1991 by Word Publishing, Dallas, Texas 75039.
Used by permission.

Scripture quotations marked NIV are taken from the *Holy Bible, New International
Version®*. NIV®. Copyright © 1973, 1978, 1984 by International Bible Society. Used by
permission of Zondervan Publishing House. All rights reserved.

Scripture quotations marked NKJV are taken from *The New King James Version*. Copyright
© 1979, 1980, 1982, Thomas Nelson, Inc.

Scripture quotations marked NLT are taken from the *Holy Bible, New Living Translation*,
copyright © 1996. Used by permission of Tyndale House Publishers, Inc., Wheaton, Illinois
60189. All rights reserved.

Cover and Interior Design by Kimberly Sagmiller, VisibilityCreative.com

ISBN: 1-4041-0494-1
ISBN 13: 1-978-140410-494-5

Published in the United States of America

inspirational insights for the path ahead

Published by

THOMAS NELSON

Since 1798

www.thomasnelson.com

$\mathcal{T}able$ OF CONTENTS

Table OF CONTENTS

Never bend your head.

Always hold it high.

Look the world straight in the eye.

HELEN KELLER

Living A Life of Boldness

We are surrounded by a great cloud of people
whose lives tell us what faith means.
So let us run the race that is before us
and never give up.

HEBREWS 12:1

Independence Day

Fear not, for I am with you;
Be not dismayed, for I am your God.
I will strengthen you,
Yes, I will help you, I will uphold you
with My righteous right hand.

Isaiah 41:10 NKJV

Life is full of starting-over days, days that often feel like a fresh taste of freedom. The choices and changes that are right around the corner seem sweet and exciting, because the direction you choose to go is now solely up to you—and God.

Being dependent on God doesn't interfere with that newfound freedom. Relying on God for guidance, strength, comfort, wisdom, and countless other gifts allows you to risk throwing yourself wholeheartedly into the adventure of life. It's like having a partner belay your rope while rock climbing. It gives you the freedom and courage to tackle higher and harder climbs. The closer the "partnership" you have with God, the freer you'll find you are to reach your true potential.

Freedom means I have been set free to become all that God wants me to be, to achieve all that God wants me to achieve, to enjoy all that God wants me to enjoy.
Warren Wiersbe

Heavenly Father,
Thank You for the freedom that comes from trusting and relying on You. Lord, as I make new plans and chart a new course, I pray that You would fill me with passion to do Your will and confidence in Your love and grace.

Amen.

Be strong and brave.
Don't be afraid of them
and don't be frightened,
because the LORD your God
will go with you.
He will not leave you
or forget you.

Deuteronomy 31:6

Bold Faith

God is looking for those who believe that what He says is more important than what anyone else says. That what He thinks is more important than what anyone else thinks. That what He wants is more important than what anyone else wants. That His will is more important than their own.

God is looking for another Noah. Another Meshach. Another Shadrach. Another Abednego.

One person with God is not alone but a majority!

ANNE GRAHAM LOTZ

Losing Your Performance Anxiety

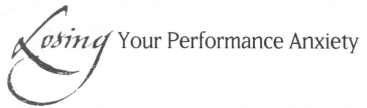

*Make every effort to give yourself to God as the kind of
person he will approve. Be a worker who is not ashamed
and who uses the true teaching in the right way.*

2 Timothy 2:15

Most people suffer from chronic performance anxiety. Is that the case with you? Are you constantly wondering what kind of reviews you will receive from your family, your boss, or your coworkers? If so, here's a little stage wisdom to help you cope.

Kill the foot lights and turn up the house lights. When you do, you will see that there is only one VIP in the audience—God. Ultimately, His review is the only one that matters. When you live your life in a manner that is pleasing to Him, it will build your confidence because it will be established on something solid, instead of on the shifting sands of people's opinions. So, chase away your anxiety and live your life for God. You're bound to be a hit with Him.

What must our natures be like
before [God] can feel at home within us?
He asks nothing but a pure heart and a single mind.
He desires but sincerity, transparency,
humility, and love.
A. W. Tozer

Heavenly Father,
You are the audience member who really counts. Help me to live a life that is pleasing to You and to look only for Your approval, not for the approval of those around me. I want to receive a standing ovation from You.

Amen.

Making Plans

To meet a goal of any kind, you need to have a concrete
understanding of what it requires—and of who you are.
God can help you do just that.

In the lines below, list some of your gifts and talents.
Then list some of your most important goals.

_____

_____

_____

_____

_____

_____

_____

_____

Let God help you evaluate potential goals that lie ahead
and see how they fit with who He created you to be.
In the coming weeks, prioritize the steps it will take
to reach your goals in a way that honors Him.

With a little prayerful planning, you're well on your
way to achieving more than you ever thought possible.

*The tragedy in life doesn't lie
in not reaching your goal.
The tragedy lies in
not having a goal to reach.*
Benjamin Mays

True Success

Trust in the Lord with all your heart and lean not on your
own understanding; in all your ways acknowledge him,
and he will make your paths straight.

Proverbs 3:5–6 NIV

Personal success cannot be measured by the make
of your car, the size of your paycheck, or even the
recognition you receive for a job well done. True success
depends on who you are, not on what you've accomplished.

God created you with a unique potential only you can fulfill.
The more you focus on becoming who God intended you
to be, the more successful you'll become—no matter what
career path you choose.

Use the gifts God's given you to the best of your ability.

Ask Him to guide you in making wise decisions. Seek His approval more than the approval of those around you. Then, your success is sure.

It is not your business to succeed, but to do right;
when you have done so, the rest lies with God.
C. S. Lewis

Heavenly Father,
Help me to tackle the challenges in front of me, not preoccupied with success but focused on doing the best I can to glorify You. Lord, thank You for the gifts that You've given me. Help me to use them to their absolute fullest.

Amen.

I tell you the truth, whoever believes in me will do the same things that I do. Those who believe will do even greater things than these.

JOHN 14:12

God takes ordinary people and enables them to do extraordinary things.

Warren W. Wiersbe

Do not be afraid;
only believe.

LUKE 8:50 NKJV

Let all your fears go—
give them to God.
He will not let you down.

Peter Marshall

Be Strong and Courageous

The LORD is my light and my salvation.
So why should I be afraid? The LORD protects me from
danger. So why should I tremble?

Psalm 27:1 NLT

It takes courage to go where God leads. He'll often take you right to the doorstep of your greatest fears, put you face-to-face with someone you can't stand to be around, or bring a situation into your life that seems impossible to work out. Don't panic. Those are the times when you can really see God's power in action.

You were never created to handle tough times alone. Consider David. The only reason he could conquer a giant was because God was with him. You have the same advantage. God is fighting every battle with you, never against you.

So take courage. Stand up to the giants in your life. With God's help, victory is at hand.

Courage faces fear and thereby masters it.
Martin Luther King, Jr.

Heavenly Father,
I know that You are strong and capable.
I also know that You care about me and want
what's best for me. Remind me of who You are, Lord,
and fill me with the courage to face the giants in my life.

Amen.

A PRAYER FOR BOLDNESS

❖ ❖ ❖ ❖ ❖ ❖ ❖ ❖ ❖ ❖ ❖ ❖ ❖ ❖ ❖ ❖

Heavenly Father,

Sometimes the weight of the future overwhelms me.
I'm not always sure which direction to turn,
which path to pursue. I'm not always sure of myself.

Lord, I know that You have prepared a bright future for me
and have a purpose for my life. I know that You will protect
and guide me. I pray for enough courage to keep my heart
focused on Your will. Make me all that You created me to
be, Lord, and enable me to charge forward with joy and
boldness on the path that You have laid out for me.

Amen.

PROMISES FROM GOD'S WORD

But the people who trust the LORD will become strong again.
They will rise up as an eagle in the sky; they will run and not
need rest; they will walk and not become tired.

Isaiah 40:31

❖ ❖ ❖ ❖ ❖ ❖ ❖ ❖ ❖ ❖ ❖ ❖ ❖ ❖ ❖ ❖ ❖ ❖

No, despite all these things, overwhelming victory is ours
through Christ, who loved us.

Romans 8:37 NLT

❖ ❖ ❖ ❖ ❖ ❖ ❖ ❖ ❖ ❖ ❖ ❖ ❖ ❖ ❖ ❖ ❖ ❖

With God's power working in us, God can do much, much
more than anything we can ask or imagine.

Ephesians 3:20

❖ ❖ ❖ ❖ ❖ ❖ ❖ ❖ ❖ ❖ ❖ ❖ ❖ ❖ ❖ ❖ ❖ ❖

Be strong and of good courage; do not be afraid, nor be
dismayed, for the LORD your God is with you wherever you go.

Joshua 1:9 NKJV

Reputation is what people think you are.

Character is what you really are.

Take care of your character

and your reputation will take care of itself.

AUTHOR UNKNOWN

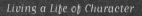
Living A Life of Character

For the righteous Lord loves justice.
The virtuous will see his face.

PSALM 11:7 NLT

Character That Holds

People with integrity walk safely,
but those who follow crooked paths will slip and fall.

Proverbs 10:9 NLT

When storms begin to blow, the integrity of a building is revealed—the strength of its foundation, the practicality of its design, and the quality of its building materials. Will it stand or will it fall?

The same holds true for your own integrity. When the pressure is on, weak spots in your faith or character readily come to light. If this happens, take note. Your integrity matures over time. If you've made unsound choices in the past, make better choices today. Make sure your foundation rests solely on what God says is true, not on what your emotions or contemporary culture says is right and fair.

Then, turn your face toward the wind with confidence. You and your integrity are built to last.

Integrity is the noblest possession.
Latin Proverb

Heavenly Father,
I know that there are flaws in my character. And I know that rather than trying to cover them up, it's much better to tackle the root of the problem. Lord, I pray that You would refine me, develop Your character in me. God, make me strong through and through, able to withstand any wind.

Amen.

The Proverb tells us, "As iron sharpens iron, so people can improve each other" (Proverbs 27:17). One of the best tools for sharpening our character is to seek out accountability and encouragement from other people.

Take a minute to prayerfully consider
the relationships in your life.
Is there someone whose wisdom you admire,
someone you might want to ask to be your mentor?
Is there someone you'd like to take under your wing?
Do you think you have the kind of close friends
who want to see you become your best?

Once you've taken stock of your relationships, think about what steps you might need to take next, and then take those steps, whether it's nurturing an existing friendship or seeking out new ones. Remember that God goes with you, and that the friendships He brings your way have the potential to make you spiritually stronger and sharper.

Be united with other Christians.
A wall with loose bricks is not good.
The bricks must be cemented together.
Corrie Ten Boom

A Constant Companion

Dear friends, we have these promises from God, so we should make ourselves pure—free from anything that makes body or soul unclean. We should try to become holy in the way we live, because we respect God.

2 Corinthians 7:1

Picture Jesus as your constant companion, accompanying you for coffee with your friends, watching a DVD with you late into the night, cheering alongside you in the bleachers at a sporting event, or dropping by a convenience store with you to pick up a magazine. Does knowing Jesus is right beside you influence the choices you make or the language you use?

If there is any part of your life you'd be embarrassed for Jesus to see or hear, your purity may be in jeopardy. It's easy to forget that God grieves when you go along with the crowd or your own less-than-pure desires or do something you know you shouldn't. Dare to do what's right. Choose to keep your heart—and life—pure.

Simplicity reaches out after God;
purity discovers and enjoys Him.
Thomas à Kempis

Heavenly Father,
Lord, I know that You are always with me. And if that's true, I know I need to live my life in a way that pleases You. Father, show me the things in my life that grieve You, and give me the wisdom and strength to turn from those things. Thank You, Lord, for Your mercy and the power to live a life that's pleasing to You.

Amen.

No, O people, the Lord has told you
what is good, and this is what he
requires of you: to do what is right,
to love mercy, and to walk
humbly with your God.

Micah 6:8 NLT

The Path to Righteousness

You're invited to live with the Lord, to make yourself at
home with Him. But there's a particular way to get there.

Walk uprightly. Work righteousness.
Speak the truth in your heart.

In short, let your life be cleansed and free and full
of all good things. Be saturated in His Spirit.

PETER WALLACE

Beautiful Honesty

An honest answer is as pleasing as a kiss on the lips.

Proverbs 24:26

You don't have to be on the FBI's Most Wanted List to be dishonest. All you have to do is exaggerate a personal story to make yourself look better in your friends' eyes. Eat a few grapes before you pay for the bunch at the grocery store. Or record your weight a few pounds lower than reality on a health insurance form.

Dishonesty is a habit that's easy to develop. Honesty is not so easy, but it is a gift to the God who loves you. It tells Him that He can trust you. It tells you that you can trust yourself. Honesty may stir up some waves on the surface of your life, but deep down in the depths of your soul, it produces genuine, lasting peace.

Honesty has a beautiful and refreshing simplicity about it. No ulterior motives. No hidden meanings.

Charles R. Swindoll

Heavenly Father,
You have taught me that truth is powerful, and that when I speak the truth, I make room for Your power in my life and in the world. Show me where I am most tempted to compromise the truth, Lord, and cultivate in me an honest spirit.

Amen.

Roots and Fruits

Good people have good things in their hearts, and so they say good things. But evil people have evil in their hearts, so they say evil things.

Matthew 12:35

An apple tree produces apples, right? You wouldn't expect it to produce watermelons or kumquats. It only produces fruit in keeping with the kind of tree it is.

Your heart is the same way. It produces words that reflect the kind of heart you have. Sure, people can fake it for a while. They can try to sound sweet and sincere when their hearts are really filled with anger or pride. But eventually that "natural" fruit is going to blossom.

Watching your words begins with examining your own

heart. Ask God if you have any negative attitudes that need pruning. With His help, you can consistently give words of love, instead of carelessly tossing rotten verbal apples.

Good words are worth much, and cost little.
George Herbert

Heavenly Father,
I pray today that You would examine my heart and help me to weed out any bad or hurtful attitudes. Fill my heart with Your goodness and allow it to overflow to my lips. May my words be pleasing to You, Lord God.

Amen.

 God's Way

Whoever serves me must follow me.
Then my servant will be with me
everywhere I am. My Father will honor
anyone who serves me.

JOHN 12:26

❖

To know Christ is to
grow into holiness.

George Hodges

❖

God loves us the way we are,
but He loves us too much
to leave us that way.

Leighton Ford

Blessed are those who keep His testimonies, who seek Him with the whole heart.

PSALM 119:2 NKJV

God orders your steps.
He points to the narrow road
rather than the broad one.

Joni Eareckson Tada

 *Living* God's Way

True Humility

Pride leads only to shame; it is wise to be humble.

Proverbs 11:2

Unlike what you see in the movies, humility is a good thing. It isn't putting yourself down or trying to blend in with the wallpaper. Humility is simply seeing yourself from God's point of view. It's accepting that you're worth no more, or less, than any other person whom God dearly loves.

Once you have a clear view of yourself, you can get a clearer view of what God wants you to do. You won't argue over what you think is too hard for you to tackle or way beneath your dignity. You can do whatever God asks—and rest in knowing that with God, your best is always good enough.

For those who would learn God's ways, humility is the first thing, humility is the second, humility is the third.
Saint Augustine

Heavenly Father,
I know that You value humility and that You have promised to exalt the humble and humble the exalted. Lord, help me see myself through Your eyes. Grant me a spirit of humility. And enable me to look to the needs of others' as much as I look to my own.

Amen.

A PRAYER FOR INTEGRITY

❖ ❖ ❖ ❖ ❖ ❖ ❖ ❖ ❖ ❖ ❖ ❖ ❖ ❖ ❖

Heavenly Father,

I know that, more than my vocational or educational success, You desire my spiritual growth and the development of my character. Help me adopt this same priority, Lord, and guard my heart against temptation.

Make me a person of discipline and righteousness. Let my actions match my words—let my conduct point others to You. Enable me to follow Your will and Your Word, today and every day.

Amen.

PROMISES FROM GOD'S WORD

Patience produces character, and character produces hope.

Romans 5:4

❖ ❖ ❖ ❖ ❖ ❖ ❖ ❖ ❖ ❖ ❖ ❖ ❖ ❖ ❖ ❖ ❖ ❖ ❖

We show we are servants of God by our pure lives.

2 Corinthians 6:6

❖ ❖ ❖ ❖ ❖ ❖ ❖ ❖ ❖ ❖ ❖ ❖ ❖ ❖ ❖ ❖ ❖ ❖ ❖

You can trust God, who will not permit you to be tempted
more than you can stand. But when you are tempted, he
will also give you a way to escape so that you will be able to
stand it.

1 Corinthians 10:13

❖ ❖ ❖ ❖ ❖ ❖ ❖ ❖ ❖ ❖ ❖ ❖ ❖ ❖ ❖ ❖ ❖ ❖ ❖

We all show the Lord's glory, and we are being changed
to be like him. This change in us brings ever greater glory,
which comes from the Lord, who is the Spirit.

2 Corinthians 3:18

❖ ❖ ❖ ❖ ❖ ❖ ❖ ❖ ❖ ❖ ❖ ❖ ❖ ❖ ❖ ❖ ❖ ❖ ❖

Respecting the LORD and not being proud will bring you
wealth, honor, and life.

Proverbs 22:4

Immortality lies not in the things you leave behind,

but in the people your life has touched.

AUTHOR UNKNOWN

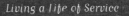

Living A Life of Service

Do not be interested only in your own life,
but be interested in the lives of others.

PHILIPPIANS 2:4

Making a Difference

Do everything without complaining or arguing. Then you will be innocent and without any wrong. You will be God's children without fault. But you are living with crooked and mean people all around you, among whom you shine like stars in the dark world.

Philippians 2:14–15 NCV

You are a walking, talking message of hope. Whether you realize it or not, your character, words, and actions are all preaching a sermon to those you meet along the road of life. The closer you follow God, the more visible He'll be to others through you.

You may never know how wide your influence really goes. An act of kindness, a word of encouragement, or a job well done could be what moves a close friend, or even a stranger, one step closer to knowing God.

Take a moment to thank God for the people who've had a positive influence on your life. Then, ask God to help you become someone else's reason for thanks.

We can influence others as much as
God has influenced us.
Bobbie-Jean Merck

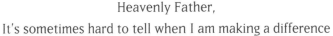

Heavenly Father,
It's sometimes hard to tell when I am making a difference in another person's life. In the midst of daily life it's easy to forget that I am a walking, talking billboard for You. Help me to be a good influence in the lives of those whom You place in my path.

Amen.

Do all the good you can,

By all the means you can,

In all the ways you can,

In all the places you can,

At all the times you can,

To all the people you can,

As long as ever you can.

John Wesley

A Helping Hand

We'll often notice things wrong with people,
but does that initial look lead to compassion and helping,
or to judging and distance? Compassion and judging
are two different ways of "seeing."

When we stop judging, we rest from the incessant
work of analyzing others. We don't need to figure out
what's wrong with people—that's God's job.
Our job is to try to understand.

PAUL E. MILLER

Compassion in Action

The LORD is good to all;
he has compassion on all he has made.

Psalm 145:9 NIV

I magine what it would be like to see the world through God's eyes. How would you feel about the woman in the wheelchair at the grocery store? The neighbor kid who just found out his parents are getting a divorce? The homeless guy on the park bench?

Seeing individuals the way God does makes you want to put love into action and help. That's compassion kicking in. Compassion doesn't just feel sorry for people, though. It strives to make a positive difference in their lives. So ask God to help you see through His eyes—and then let you know how to help. Even if the only action you can take is to pray, your compassion can make a difference in the world.

God's care will carry you so you can carry others.
Robert H. Schuller

Heavenly Father,
Sometimes compassion is hard for me—it's hard to notice the needs around me, and I don't always see people the way You do. Today I pray for Your compassion. Remind me of how You have had mercy on me, Lord, show me the mercy You have for others, and give me wisdom to know how to help them.

Amen.

How to Develop a Vision for Your Future

Look inside.

What do you feel most passionate about?

_____

_____

_____

_____

Look behind.

What have you learned?

What experiences have affected you most deeply?

_____

_____

_____

_____

Look around.

What resources are available to you?

What needs do you see that you desperately want to meet?

_____

_____

_____

_____

Look up.

What does God want for your life?

_____

_____

_____

_____

In the great orchestra we call life,
you have an instrument and a song,
and you owe it to God to play them both sublimely.
Max Lucado

The Value of Mercy

He has showed you, O man, what is good. And what does the LORD require of you? To act justly and to love mercy and to walk humbly with your God.

Micah 6:8 NIV

Mercy is the key that sets a prisoner free. It extends grace in place of judgment, forgiveness in place of punishment, honor in place of disdain. It makes no sense, except to a heart filled with God's unconditional love.

Mercy is a gift God asks you to give to others—not because they deserve it, but because of the mercy God has demonstrated in your own life. Ask God to bring to mind anyone who could use a tender touch of mercy. Depending on how God leads you to bestow this special gift, the one who receives it may never even be fully aware of its extent.

But you will. You'll find that being merciful frees up your own heart to love more authentically.

Nothing graces the Christian soul as much as mercy.
Saint Ambrose

Heavenly Father,
Thank You so much for the mercy You bestow upon me every day. I pray that You would awaken me to that mercy and help me see it more clearly so that I can pass it on to the people You bring across my path. Give me opportunities to show the world what mercy looks like, Lord.

Amen.

You are the light of the world—like a
city on a hilltop that cannot be hidden.

MATTHEW 5:14 NLT

*You don't have to be like the world to
have an impact on the world.*

Max Lucado

My children, we should love people not only with words and talk, but by our actions and true caring.

1 JOHN 3:18

The willing feet that go on errands of love, work for Christ.

Arthur Ingram

Shout It from the Rooftops

Through Christ, God made peace between us and himself,
and God gave us the work of telling everyone about the
peace we can have with him.

2 Corinthians 5:18

When we survey the world around us, we see a world that's hurting. Sin and suffering surround us on every corner. The world needs to hear the message of God's saving love in Jesus. As believers in Christ, we know how He has touched our hearts and changed our lives. Now is the time to share our personal testimonies with others.

The old familiar hymn begins, "What a friend we have in Jesus." No truer words were ever written. Jesus is the sovereign friend and ultimate savior of humanity. Christ showed enduring love for His believers by willingly sacrificing His own life so that we might have eternal life. Let us love Him, praise Him, and share His message of salvation with our neighbors—and the world.

Witnessing is not something that we do for the Lord;
it is something that He does through us if we are filled
with the Holy Spirit.
Warren Wiersbe

Heavenly Father,
I know that You have a message of hope and healing for the world, and that You want to use me to deliver that message. Fill me with Your words and with the courage to share Your truth with others, Lord. May I be a message of love from You to the world.

Amen.

A PRAYER FOR A SPIRIT OF SERVICE

❖ ❖ ❖ ❖ ❖ ❖ ❖ ❖ ❖ ❖ ❖ ❖ ❖ ❖ ❖ ❖ ❖

Heavenly Father,

I know that You love every person on the earth just as much
as You love me, and that You have a message of healing and
restoration for them.

God, enable me to carry that message throughout my sphere
of influence. Guide me as I seek out people to reach with
Your healing love, and help me make decisions and plans
based on serving others. I pray that You would use me, God,
use my life to make a difference for Your kingdom.

Amen.

PROMISES FROM GOD'S WORD

But when the Holy Spirit comes to you, you will receive power. You will be my witnesses—in Jerusalem, in all of Judea, in Samaria, and in every part of the world.   Acts 1:8

❖ ❖ ❖ ❖ ❖ ❖ ❖ ❖ ❖ ❖ ❖ ❖ ❖ ❖ ❖ ❖ ❖ ❖ ❖

I tell you the truth, anything you did for even the least of my people here, you also did for me.   Matthew 25:40

❖ ❖ ❖ ❖ ❖ ❖ ❖ ❖ ❖ ❖ ❖ ❖ ❖ ❖ ❖ ❖ ❖ ❖ ❖

God is fair; he will not forget the work you did and the love you showed for him by helping his people. And he will remember that you are still helping them.   Hebrews 6:10

❖ ❖ ❖ ❖ ❖ ❖ ❖ ❖ ❖ ❖ ❖ ❖ ❖ ❖ ❖ ❖ ❖ ❖ ❖

Religion that God accepts as pure and without fault is this: caring for orphans or widows who need help, and keeping yourself free from the world's evil influence.   James 1:27

❖ ❖ ❖ ❖ ❖ ❖ ❖ ❖ ❖ ❖ ❖ ❖ ❖ ❖ ❖ ❖ ❖ ❖ ❖

May our Lord Jesus Christ himself and God our Father encourage you and strengthen you in every good thing you do and say.   2 Thessalonians 2:16–17

God always gives his very best

to those who leave the choice with him.

JAMES HUDSON TAYLOR

Living A Life of Optimism

My future is in your hands.

PSALM 31:15 NLT

 God's Way

Good Days Ahead

*With God's power working in us, God can do much, much
more than anything we can ask or imagine.*

Ephesians 3:20

You've been waiting for months for the release of the
sequel to your favorite movie. Finally, the time has
come. You've waited in line, purchased your ticket, and
found yourself a seat. You have an idea of what lies ahead,
but you don't know exactly what's going to happen. All you
know is that it's bound to be great.

That's the kind of expectation you can have about the life
God has planned for you. He is more creative than any
filmmaker, more amazing than any special effect, and more
wonderful than any cinematic hero. You may not fully
understand your story's beauty until you've reached the

finale, but God promises every detail of the plot has been chosen for your ultimate good.

We block Christ's advance in our lives by failure of expectation.
William Temple

Heavenly Father,
Sometimes when I think about what the future might hold, I slip into worry. I forget that You have a plan for my life, and that You are trustworthy beyond my wildest imagination. Thank You for both the good days and the hard days ahead, and thank You that You have a good future in store for me.

Amen.

GPS for Life

The LORD says, "I will make you wise and show you where
to go. I will guide you and watch over you."

Psalm 32:8

A Global Positioning System for your life would make a great gift. You could type in your goals—where you want to go—and a friendly voice would advise you as to the best way to get there.

Your relationship with God is better than any GPS on the market. God knows where you've been, where you are, and which direction is best for you to head in the future. He wants you to have access to that same useful information. By reading the Bible, weighing advice from godly friends, and asking God's Spirit to guide you in prayer, you have access to a system of guidance that will never fail, no matter where you roam.

I know not the way God leads me,
but well do I know my Guide.
Martin Luther

Heavenly Father,
You are better than any GPS man could ever create. You know better than anyone else the best path for my life. Help me to hear Your voice clearly so that You can point me in the right direction. As I follow Your will for my life, I know You will guide me where I need to go.

Amen.

Prayer Power

As you take the next steps in your journey,
remember to take those steps with God.
And remember to pray.

Prayer changes things, and it changes you.

Today, instead of turning things over in your mind,
turn them over to God in prayer.

Instead of worrying about your next decision,
decide to let God lead the way.

Don't limit your prayers to meals or bedtime.

Pray constantly about things great and small.
God is listening, and He wants to hear from you now.

ജ ജ ജ ജ ജ ജ ജ ജ

Prayer does not change God;
it changes me.
C. S. Lewis

ജ ജ ജ ജ ജ ജ ജ ജ

Finding Your Life's Word

Each person has his own gift from God.
One has one gift, another has another gift.

1 Corinthians 7:7

A career is defined as a profession or vocation. It's more than just a job. Your career is your life's work. It should be something you love, something you feel you were born to do. Sounds simple—but it isn't always so easy to put your finger on. If you feel that way, you aren't alone. Many people stop and start a few times before they find their truest calling.

No matter what, don't settle for less. Keep looking and trying new things until you find the proper career path for you. You'll know it by the little leap your heart takes when you think and pray about it. You'll know because God will confirm it to you deep inside. Life is too short to spend it doing anything but what God has called you to do.

No life can be dreary when work is delight.
Frances Ridley Havergal

Heavenly Father,
I don't want to settle for anything less than what You have called me to do. Help me to find the right career path that will tap into my specific gifts and talents. As I step out into the world, guide my steps—and my heart—and let me know when I have found what You have created me to do.

Amen.

The LORD is my shepherd;

I have everything I need.

He lets me rest in green pastures.

He leads me to calm water.

He gives me new strength.

Psalm 23:1–3

In God's Hands

Once we give ourselves up to God, shall we attempt to get
hold of what can never belong to us—*tomorrow?*
Our lives are His, our times in His hand. He is Lord over
what will happen, never mind what may happen.
When we prayed "Thy will be done," did we suppose
He did not hear us? He heard indeed, and daily makes our
business His. If my life is once surrendered, all is well.
Let me not grab it back, as though it were in peril in His hand
but would be safer in mine!

ELISABETH ELLIOT

Brand~New Beginnings

The LORD says, "I, I am the One who forgives all your
sins, for my sake; I will not remember your sins."
Isaiah 43:25

Many situations in life—graduation, starting a new job, moving out on your own—are brand-new beginnings, a fresh start, a chance to try again or to try something completely new.

These aren't the only fresh starts you'll experience in life, however. God offers you a "beginning-again" ceremony every time you need a second chance. Whenever you blow it, make a poor choice, or even all-out rebel, God says, "Let's begin again." You don't have to go to a job interview or sign a new lease. All God asks is that you come to Him in honest repentance and ask His forgiveness. From that moment, the

past truly is history. All is forgiven and your fresh start is
ready to commence.

*I like sunrises, Mondays, and new seasons. God seems to
be saying, "With me you can always start fresh."*
Ada Lum

Heavenly Father,
Thank You so much for Your gift of a second chance, a fresh
start. No matter how many new beginnings I have in my life,
Your forgiveness and grace are more than I could ever need.
Help me to come to You every time I need to begin again; I
know You will always be there waiting.

Amen.

The Lord directs the steps of the godly.
He delights in every detail of their lives.

PSALM 37:23 NLT

❖

*Obey God one step at a time, then the
next step will come into view.*

Catherine Marshall

❖

*Even in the winter, even in the midst
of the storm, the sun is still there.
Somewhere, up above the clouds, it
still shines and warms and pulls at
the life buried deep inside the brown
branches and frozen earth. The sun is
there! Spring will come.*

Gloria Gaither

Eye has not seen, nor ear heard,
nor have entered into the
heart of man the things
which God has prepared
for those who love Him.
1 CORINTHIANS 2:9 NKJV

❖

*Faith expects from
God what is beyond
all expectation.*
Andrew Murray

Holding onto Hope

*But we are hoping for something we do not have yet,
and we are waiting for it patiently.*

Romans 8:25

Hope is the perfect life preserver in the midst of any storm. It helps keep your head above water, enabling you to fight off feelings of discouragement and despair. As you catch an occasional glimpse of what lies beyond the waves, it aids in reminding you that help is on the way, even if you can't quite see it yet. Hope helps you survive.

When storm clouds are gathering on the horizon, or if a torrential downpour has caught you by surprise, hold fast to hope. Remember how God came through time and time again for people in the Bible. Think about how He's come through for you. Then, meditate on His steadfast promises, your greatest source of hope. Help is on its way.

Do not look to your hope,
but to Christ, your source of hope.
Charles Spurgeon

Heavenly Father,
I know that You are always faithful, and that the hope I have in You is steadfast and immovable. Thank You for the assurance that You have a bright future for me. Today, Lord, as I'm facing difficulties, remind me of Your promises and fill my heart with hope.

Amen.

A Prayer of Hope for the Future

❖ ❖ ❖ ❖ ❖ ❖ ❖ ❖ ❖ ❖ ❖ ❖ ❖ ❖ ❖ ❖

Heavenly Father,

You've placed so many hopes and dreams in my heart, and I want to get started on everything right away. Give me wisdom, though, to wait for Your green light.

You know better than I do what lies ahead. Help me trust in Your great plan for my life, and when I make a mistake, please work everything together for my good. Show me Your will, and I will follow it, because I know that trusting You will bring a future more wonderful than I can imagine.

Amen.

Promises from God's Word

The LORD will always lead you. He will satisfy your
needs in dry lands and give strength to your bones.
You will be like a garden that has much water,
like a spring that never runs dry.

Isaiah 58:11

❖ ❖ ❖ ❖ ❖ ❖ ❖ ❖ ❖ ❖ ❖ ❖ ❖ ❖ ❖ ❖ ❖

Commit to the LORD whatever you do,
and your plans will succeed.

Proverbs 16:3 NIV

❖ ❖ ❖ ❖ ❖ ❖ ❖ ❖ ❖ ❖ ❖ ❖ ❖ ❖ ❖ ❖ ❖

"I know what I am planning for you," says the LORD.
"I have good plans for you, not plans to hurt you.
I will give you hope and a good future."

Jeremiah 29:11

❖ ❖ ❖ ❖ ❖ ❖ ❖ ❖ ❖ ❖ ❖ ❖ ❖ ❖ ❖ ❖ ❖

You guide me with your advice,
and later you will receive me in honor.

Psalm 73:24

He who is filled with love is filled with God himself.

SAINT AUGUSTINE

Living A Life of Love

All of you should be in agreement,
understanding each other,
loving each other as a family,
being kind and humble.

I PETER 3:8

What Love Looks Like

No one has ever seen God, but if we love each other,
God lives in us, and his love is made perfect in us.
1 John 4:12

Want to know what love looks like? Look at God. Consider His sacrifice, His patience, His comfort, His faithfulness, His generosity. God's creativity in expressing love is so great that it's almost incomprehensible.

Consider how your love stands up next to His. Don't get discouraged. You're not God. At times, your love still falters and fails—but God's love is always at work in your life. He's helping you love others in the same wonderful way He so deeply loves you.

Let God's creative compassion inspire you to love others

well. Ask for His help in knowing the best way to express your love so that it meets needs, builds relationships, and warms hearts. Then, take a moment to sit back and enjoy His love for you.

If we have the true love of God in our hearts,
we will show it in our lives.
D.L. Moody

Heavenly Father,
Thank You for Your amazing love that teaches me how to love other people. I want to love others the way that You love them. Help me find ways to reach out to them and express my love in ways that people need it the most.

Amen.

Christ's love is greater
than anyone can ever know,
but I pray that you
will be able to know that love.
Then you can be filled
with the fullness of God.

Ephesians 3:19

Our True Selves

The unconditional love we so desperately need if we are to become authentic comes only from God. Interestingly enough, it is when we let God love us unconditionally at a deep level that we tend to become the person He really wants us to be. It is only when we feel His total love for us that we are free to be genuine in all of our relations with others. This genuineness, I feel confident, is exactly what pleases Him most.

NEIL CLARK WARREN

Being an Encourager

May our Lord Jesus Christ himself and God our Father encourage you and strengthen you in every good thing you do and say.

2 Thessalonians 2:16–17

Encouragement is more than building others up with your words. It's helping them find the courage to move ahead in a positive direction.

When God opens your eyes to someone who's discouraged, disappointed, or in need of comfort, ask Him for the wisdom to know the best words and actions to share. Then, let God's love for you encourage your own heart so that you can reach out in confidence, kindness, and humility.

Whatever you do or say, remember that it's God's love and power working through you that ultimately help another person—not your own superior counseling abilities. When God uses you in the lives of others, always thank Him for the privilege of being an encourager.

> *One of the highest of human duties*
> *is the duty of encouragement.*
> William Barclay

Heavenly Father,
I have been encouraged so that I might be an encouragement to people. Use me to help the people You place in my life. Place Your words in my mouth so that the things I say will bring encouragement to others. I want to be Your hands and feet to those who need Your love.

Amen.

Across the Miles

Jesus said, "Greater love has no one than this,
than to lay down one's life for his friends."

John 15:13 NKJV

Events like graduation day, a big move, or a new job can
bring excitement, change, expectation—and good-byes.
A lot of the people you've grown close to over the past
several years may not be headed the same direction that
God is leading you. But that doesn't mean your friendships
can't continue to grow.

Keeping in touch across the miles takes effort. However,
an e-mail, a crazy card, or a heartfelt phone call is all a
friendship needs to spark many happy reunions. The friends
God brings into your life are worth holding onto—and
praying for. That includes the ones you haven't met yet.

Along with those good-byes, you're also going to be saying a lot of glad-to-meet-yous. So open your heart. Some of your very best friends are waiting to meet you.

Friendship is one of the sweetest joys of life.
Many might have failed beneath the bitterness of
their trial had they not found a friend.
Charles Spurgeon

Heavenly Father,
I know that relationships are one of the most important things in life. God, right now I pray over my friendships and ask You to guide them and cause them to thrive. Show me how to encourage and bless the friends I have, and be with me as I forge new relationships.

Amen.

Making an Investment

Building good relationships takes effort.

Think about the most important people in your life.
Then think of something to do
to nurture those relationships.

Call a friend to see if she wants to grab coffee this week;
set a movie date with your siblings.

Investing a little time and energy will pay off
with a deeper, better relationship—
the kind that makes life richer and happier.

෯ ෯ ෯ ෯ ෯ ෯ ෯ ෯

There is nothing on this earth
more to be prized than true friendship.
Saint Thomas Aquinas

෯ ෯ ෯ ෯ ෯ ෯ ෯ ෯

A Common Bond

If we live in the light, as God is in the light,
we can share fellowship with each other.

1 John 1:7

"Fellowship" is an old-fashioned-sounding word, bringing
to mind potlucks—complete with fat-laden casseroles
and colorful gelatin salads—eaten in church basement
fellowship halls. But true fellowship is never out of date. It's
people living on the cutting edge of community, sharing life
together.

When Christ is the center of that life, that common bond
is more than friendship. It's a love that matures through
differences and struggle, as well as through praise and play.

To experience fellowship, you have to involve your life with the lives of other people who believe in Christ. You need to risk being real and work your way through problems instead of running from them. Only then can you experience the joy that being part of God's family brings.

No man is an island, entire of itself; every man is a piece of the continent, a part of the main.

John Donne

Heavenly Father,
Thank You for true fellowship that is centered on You and Your family. That kind of fellowship endures and matures, no matter what circumstances life may bring. Help me to continue to involve my life with the lives of Your people, and receive the joy that such fellowship brings.

Amen.

If we love one another,
God abides in us, and His love
has been perfected in us.

1 JOHN 4:12 NKJV

Life minus love equals nothing.

George Sweeting

By helping each other with
your troubles, you truly obey
the law of Christ.

GALATIANS 6:2

*Life becomes harder for us when we
live for others, but it also becomes
richer and happier.*

Albert Schweitzer

Gentle Giant

Always be humble, gentle, and patient,
accepting each other in love.

Ephesians 4:2

Remember wrestling on the floor when you were a
kid? The inevitable parental warning usually went
something like this: "Don't play rough or someone's going
to get hurt!" That same warning holds true today. Anytime
you interact with another person, there's a chance someone
may get hurt. That's why being gentle with one another is so
important.

It doesn't matter if you're a big, burly guy or a gal who's
never met a risk she didn't want to take. Gentleness is not a
personality trait. It's a character quality worth putting into
practice.

Whomever you spend time with today, friends and strangers alike, play gently. Let your words, your tone of voice, your actions, and even your attitude reflect a tender, godly spirit.

Nothing is so strong as gentleness,
nothing so gentle as real strength.
Saint Francis de Sales

Heavenly Father,
Thank You for Your gentleness in dealing with me, and thank You for the people in my life who model that same gentleness. Lord, teach me to be gentle. Teach me to help and heal others with my words and show them Your love with my actions.

Amen.

A PRAYER FOR A LOVING HEART

❖ ❖ ❖ ❖ ❖ ❖ ❖ ❖ ❖ ❖ ❖ ❖ ❖ ❖ ❖

Heavenly Father,

Sometimes I do all the right things, but with an unloving attitude. And sometimes I fail to show love at all—I get caught up in my schedule or get stressed out, and I snap in frustration at a friend or forget to stop and listen to someone I care about.

I remember now that all of the "good" things I do for You actually count as nothing if I'm not sharing Your love with the people You've placed in my life. Please forgive my attitude and fill my heart with love, kindness, and consideration for everyone I meet.

Amen.

Promises from God's Word

No one has ever seen God, but if we love each other, God
lives in us, and his love is made perfect in us.

1 John 4:12

❖ ❖ ❖ ❖ ❖ ❖ ❖ ❖ ❖ ❖ ❖ ❖ ❖ ❖ ❖ ❖ ❖

Most importantly, love each other deeply, because love will
cause people to forgive each other for many sins.

1 Peter 4:8

❖ ❖ ❖ ❖ ❖ ❖ ❖ ❖ ❖ ❖ ❖ ❖ ❖ ❖ ❖ ❖ ❖

If two or three people come together in my name,
I am there with them.

Matthew 18:20

❖ ❖ ❖ ❖ ❖ ❖ ❖ ❖ ❖ ❖ ❖ ❖ ❖ ❖ ❖ ❖ ❖

Christ himself is our peace.

Ephesians 2:14

 God's Way

If the only prayer you said

in your whole life was, "thank you,"

that would suffice.

MEISTER ECKHART

Living A Life of Gratitude

So then, just as you received Christ Jesus as Lord,
continue to live in him, rooted and built up in him,
strengthened in the faith as you were taught,
and overflowing with thankfulness.

COLOSSIANS 2:6–7 NIV

A Thankful Heart

Be thankful in all circumstances, for this is God's will for
you who belong to Christ Jesus.

1 Thessalonians 5:18 NLT

You don't need a turkey to celebrate Thanksgiving. All
you need is a reason. And God has given you more
reasons to be thankful than He's created stars in the sky, so
why wait?

Start with what you see—the clothes you're wearing, the
food in the fridge, the beauty of a summer day. Then think
about the people you love and how they've touched your
life. Next, consider what God has given you that can't be
held in your hands—things like hope, forgiveness, and your
future home in heaven. Sit quietly as God brings to mind
even more reasons to say thank you.

Stopping to say thanks will remind you of how big God is and how good your life is, no matter what kind of day you're having.

No duty is more urgent than that of returning thanks.
Saint Ambrose

Heavenly Father,
I just want to take a minute to thank You. Lord, You continually, abundantly bless me. Most of all, thank You for the gift of Your presence.

Amen.

Blessed with Every Blessing

*Do not worry about anything but pray and ask God for
everything you need, always giving thanks. And God's
peace which is so great we cannot understand it, will
keep your hearts and minds in Christ Jesus.*

Philippians 4:6-7

When you think about counting your blessings, your
mind most likely turns to those you can see—a warm
place to live, food in the fridge, friends and family to hold
you close. But, the blessings that God showers on you every
day go far beyond what you can touch with your hands.

God's blessings include miracles like the process of prayer, a
future home in heaven, and God's ultimate gift of salvation.
Although blessings like these are really more than the human
mind can understand, they are also easily taken for granted.

Take time right now to send God a heartfelt thank-you note via prayer. Ask Him to help your gratitude grow by making you increasingly more aware of every blessing He brings your way.

The more we count the blessings we have,
the less we crave the luxuries we haven't.
William Arthur Ward

Heavenly Father,
Thank You for all of the blessings that You pour out on my life every day—both the obvious blessings I can see and touch with my hands and the less obvious ones, the many spiritual blessings I have in Christ. Help my gratitude to grow as I count my blessings each day.

Amen.

Praise be to the God and Father
of our Lord Jesus Christ.
In Christ, God has given
us every spiritual blessing
in the heavenly world.

Ephesians 1:3

Blessings in the Now

With God, there is only the infinite NOW. Therefore, by faith we must grasp the fact that all the blessings we shall ever need are already deposited in the Treasury of Heaven.

Money in any checking account will stay right there until the owner cashes a check *in the present.* Even so, we shall receive God's blessings only as we claim them one by one *in the present.* Faith in the future tense is hope—not faith. A sure sign that our hope has passed into faith is when we stop begging God and begin thanking Him for the answer to our prayer.

CATHERINE MARSHALL

Living God's Way

The Greatest Gift

He has delivered us from the power of darkness and conveyed us into the kingdom of the Son of His love, in whom we have redemption through His blood, the forgiveness of sins.

Colossians 1:13–14 NKJV

Imagine receiving a gift so overly generous that it leaves you speechless. You've done nothing to earn it. As a matter of fact, at times you've been downright awful to the one who's giving it to you. How does your heart respond?

The forgiveness of God is just such a gift. Your response to that gift—whether you apologize for the past and accept forgiveness with open arms or bury your head in shame and refuse to take what you don't deserve—is your gift to God. Which will it be?

Right now, kneel before the Giver of all good gifts. Meditate on what He's forgiven in your life and what it cost for Him to offer that free gift to you.

Jesus loves us with fidelity, purity, constancy, and passion, no matter how imperfect we are.
Stormie Omartian

Heavenly Father,
I bow before You, thanking You wholeheartedly for Your forgiveness. I have failed in so many ways, yet You always give me a second chance. Thank You for the gift of Your Son, Jesus, who paid the price for that forgiveness.

Amen.

Let God Take the Credit

As you anticipate an exciting new chapter in your life,
remember: The coming chapter, like every other,
begins and ends with God and with His Son.

God will touch your heart and guide your steps—if you let
Him. So dedicate this day to God's purpose and give thanks
for His grace. Take a minute to write a note of thanks to
God, celebrating the good things about your life right now
and in the future, and expressing your gratitude. Tuck the
note in your Bible or journal so you can look back at it often.

This is the day the Lord has created—give thanks to the One
who created it, and use it to the glory of His kingdom.

෨ ෨ ෨ ෨ ෨ ෨ ෨ ෨

The greatest honor you can give Almighty God
is to live gladly and joyfully
because of the knowledge of His love.
Juliana of Norwich

෨ ෨ ෨ ෨ ෨ ෨ ෨ ෨

He did not spare his own Son but gave him for us all. So with Jesus, God will surely give us all things.

ROMANS 8:32

We give thanks for unknown blessings already on their way.

Irish Prayer

For the LORD God is a sun and shield;
the LORD bestows favor and honor; no
good thing does he withhold from those
whose walk is blameless.

PSALM 84:11 NIV

*God made this world, this life,
for us to enjoy. Get busy with all
He has for you!*

Letting Go of the "If Onlys"

*I have learned to be satisfied with the things
I have and with everything that happens.*

Philippians 4:11

How much is enough? To a contented heart, it's as much as God has chosen to provide. To measure your personal level of contentment, complete this sentence: *I would be content if only . . . .*

What are the "if onlys" in your life? More money? Being involved in a serious relationship? Losing or gaining weight? Landing the job of your dreams?

There's another name for "if onlys." They're called idols. When your desires move from "it would be nice" to "I can't be happy without," you've chosen to believe some*thing* can satisfy you, instead of Some*one*. Ask God to reveal any "if onlys" you need to confront. Then, ask Him to show you how to find contentment where you are and with what you have right now.

God is most glorified in us when
we are most satisfied in Him.
John Piper

Heavenly Father,
You are the true satisfaction of my life. I can let go of any "if onlys" I have been holding onto and instead look to You to bring true contentment to my soul. I know that the things of this earth won't truly satisfy me—but I can find real contentment right now in my relationship with You.

Amen.

A Prayer of Thanks

❖ ❖ ❖ ❖ ❖ ❖ ❖ ❖ ❖ ❖ ❖ ❖ ❖ ❖ ❖

Heavenly Father,

Your gifts are so amazing! Thank You for Your beautiful creation, for songs that move my heart, for arms to hold my loved ones close. You bless me in ways too many to count.

I don't express my gratitude to You nearly often enough. Every day that I wake up is a new day to experience Your mercy, grace, and love. Thank You so much for this challenging, mysterious, grand, and glorious life you have planned for me!

Amen.

PROMISES FROM GOD'S WORD

The LORD's love never ends; his mercies never stop.
They are new every morning; LORD, your loyalty is great.

Lamentations 3:22–23

❖ ❖ ❖ ❖ ❖ ❖ ❖ ❖ ❖ ❖ ❖ ❖ ❖ ❖ ❖ ❖ ❖ ❖

Your love continues forever;
your loyalty goes on and on like the sky.

Psalm 89:2

❖ ❖ ❖ ❖ ❖ ❖ ❖ ❖ ❖ ❖ ❖ ❖ ❖ ❖ ❖ ❖ ❖ ❖

My God will use his wonderful riches in Christ Jesus
to give you everything you need.

Philippians 4:19

❖ ❖ ❖ ❖ ❖ ❖ ❖ ❖ ❖ ❖ ❖ ❖ ❖ ❖ ❖ ❖ ❖ ❖

Therefore I tell you, whatever you ask for in prayer, believe
that you have received it, and it will be yours.

Mark 11:24 NIV

Common sense suits itself

to the ways of the world.

Wisdom tries to conform

to the ways of heaven.

JOSEPH JOUBERT

Living A Life of Wisdom

Wisdom begins with respect for the LORD;
those who obey his orders have good understanding.

PSALM 111:10

Embracing Wisdom

*As a tree produces fruit, wisdom gives life to those who
use it, and everyone who uses it will be happy.*

Proverbs 3:18

Y ou don't have to be old to be wise. A lot of old people
do really stupid things. But then again, so do a lot of
young people. Being wise has less to do with age and IQ than
with your ability to apply what God has taught you to your
everyday life. Application takes thought, prayer, and effort.

But, to apply something, first you have to know it. As you
read the Bible, ask God to help you understand what His
words meant to the people they were originally written for,
then for you individually. (A "life application" or study Bible
can help.) Then, put what God teaches you into practice. The

more you do, the wiser you—and your actions—will become.

Men may acquire knowledge,
but wisdom is a gift direct from God.
Bob Jones

Heavenly Father,
I know there's a difference between being smart—having
a lot of head knowledge—and being wise—making right
choices. Help me to grow in wisdom each day. As Your Word
promises, making wise choices will not only save me from
harm, it will also bring me lasting peace.

Amen.

Your word is a lamp to my feet
And a light to my path.

Psalm 119:105 NKJV

Supernatural Wisdom

God alone is the Source of all wisdom.

A person may have natural logic. He or she may have
natural wisdom. But logic and wisdom err in that
they will always put the individual person first.
They are not supernatural wisdom.

Supernatural wisdom comes only from God,
and it comes through Jesus Christ—
the personification of God's wisdom to us.

LARRY LEA

Asking for God's Advice

*You guide me with your advice,
and later you will receive me in honor.*

Psalm 73:24

When you're faced with a tough decision, it's only
natural to go to a friend for advice. Chatting openly
with someone who knows you and your situation well can
help you put the pros and cons of your options into clearer
perspective. So, what could make more sense than spending
time talking things over with the One who knows you better
than anyone else?

God cares about the direction in which your life is headed.
The decisions you make each day help determine that
direction. Weighing your decisions by what's written in the

Bible and using the wisdom that God provides for the asking will not only help you determine right from wrong, but better from best.

We make our decisions, and then our decisions turn around and make us.
Francis Boreham

Heavenly Father,
The Bible tells me that when I need wisdom, all I need to do is ask, and You will gladly help me know which decision to make. Thank You for Your care for my life and that You love me more than anyone else does. I am determined to make my choices according to Your Word and with the wisdom that comes only from You.

Amen.

The Keys to Wisdom

Want to be wise?
Scripture gives us two keys to finding wisdom.

First of all, Proverbs tells us that the fear of the Lord is
the beginning of all wisdom (9:10). The first step to finding
wisdom is to develop the habit of acknowledging God. Each
morning this week, pause and pray, thanking God for His
blessings, acknowledging that He is the giver of all your gifts,
and committing your day to Him.

The Bible also teaches that God freely gives wisdom to those
who ask—"But if any of you needs wisdom, you should ask
God for it. He is generous and enjoys giving to all people, so
he will give you wisdom" (James 1:5). Before you set out on
your journey to find wisdom, simply ask God to lead you and
direct your path.

The thing to remember about wisdom is that it's all about God. Center your pursuit of wisdom around Him, and you're sure to find success.

*Wisdom begins with respect for the Lord,
and understanding begins with knowing the Holy One.*

Proverbs 9:10

Feeding Your Soul

Delight yourself also in the LORD,
And He shall give you the desires of your heart.

Psalm 37:4 NKJV

Think about that feeling of satisfaction you get when you've eaten a good meal of your favorite foods and you wisely choose to stop eating before you go from full to stuffed.

That's how God wants you to feel about life. A job well done, a dream fulfilled, a relationship healed, a confidence in knowing how much God loves you. There are numerous things God can bring your way that satisfy your heart.

God knows every one of your deepest desires. Trying to fill

these desires on your own can lead to frustration—or even lead you away from God. But letting God fill your desires in His way and in His time leads to satisfaction that lasts.

*Fulfillment comes as a by-product of our love for God.
And that satisfaction is better than we ever imagined.
God can make the pieces of this world's puzzle
fit together; he helps us view the world
from a new perspective.*
Erwin W. Lutzer

Heavenly Father,
You know my deepest desires, the things I most deeply hunger for. Thank You for Your promise to satisfy those desires with good things; things that will build me up, not tear me down. Things that will draw us closer and feed the hunger in my soul. Help me entrust my every desire to You.

Amen.

Living God's Way

Secrets of Success

Part of wisdom is stepping back for a minute
and observing how the world works.

Think back on the last five years.

What were your successes?
What were your failures?

Based on your experiences and those of others,
what would you list as the secrets to godly success?

_____

_____

_____

_____

_____

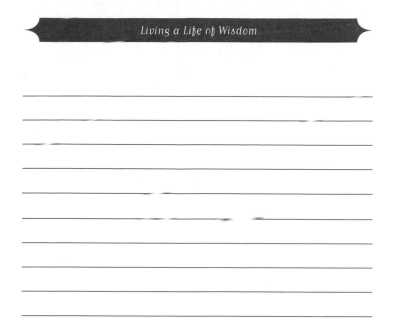

If you lack knowledge, go to school.
If you lack wisdom, get on your knees.
Vance Havner

Hold on to wisdom, and it will take care of you. Love it, and it will keep you safe.

PROVERBS 4:6

If you make the wrong choice, you will have to pay the consequences. But if you make the right choice, you receive all of the benefits.

Billy Graham

Listen carefully to wisdom; set your
mind on understanding.

PROVERBS 2:2

*Learning sleeps and snores in
libraries, but wisdom is everywhere,
wide awake, on tiptoe.*

Josh Billings

Help!

The LORD has heard my cry for help;
the LORD will answer my prayer.

Psalm 6:9

We all need a little help sometimes. Sometimes the
wisest thing we can do is whisper a short, one-word
prayer: *Help!*

Such brevity doesn't bother God. He knows exactly what's
behind your desperate plea. He also knows exactly what you
need—and it may differ considerably from what you want.
You may want circumstances to change immediately, even
time to reverse itself.

Though God can and does work miracles, usually His help
comes in subtler ways—through a renewal of strength, an

outpouring of hope, or a peace that passes understanding. It may come through the words of a friend, the kindness of a stranger, or the awesome wonder of a thunderstorm. The help God offers varies from situation to situation. But one thing that never varies is God's dependability in answering your heartfelt prayer.

Lord, help me to remember that nothing is going to
happen to me today that you and I cannot handle.
Author Unknown

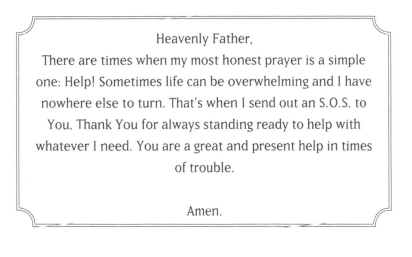

Heavenly Father,
There are times when my most honest prayer is a simple one: Help! Sometimes life can be overwhelming and I have nowhere else to turn. That's when I send out an S.O.S. to You. Thank You for always standing ready to help with whatever I need. You are a great and present help in times of trouble.

Amen.

A PRAYER FOR WISDOM

❖ ❖ ❖ ❖ ❖ ❖ ❖ ❖ ❖ ❖ ❖ ❖ ❖ ❖ ❖

Heavenly Father,

In all my years of school, I've gained a lot of head knowledge. But all that I've learned won't do me any good if I don't have the ability to apply it to my real life. I need Your wisdom for that, Lord. You are the teacher I need as I put my knowledge to work.

Each day, I pray that You will guide me in making the right choices. Only You can help me lead a balanced life. Please show me how to keep my priorities straight and use what I've learned for Your glory.

Amen.

PROMISES FROM GOD'S WORD

Those who love your teachings will find true peace,
and nothing will defeat them.

Psalm 119:165

❖ ❖ ❖ ❖ ❖ ❖ ❖ ❖ ❖ ❖ ❖ ❖ ❖ ❖ ❖ ❖ ❖ ❖ ❖

If you go the wrong way—to the right or to the left—
you will hear a voice behind you saying, "This is the right
way. You should go this way."

Isaiah 30:21

❖ ❖ ❖ ❖ ❖ ❖ ❖ ❖ ❖ ❖ ❖ ❖ ❖ ❖ ❖ ❖ ❖ ❖ ❖

But if any of you needs wisdom, you should ask God for
it. He is generous to everyone and will give you wisdom
without criticizing you.

James 1:5

❖ ❖ ❖ ❖ ❖ ❖ ❖ ❖ ❖ ❖ ❖ ❖ ❖ ❖ ❖ ❖ ❖ ❖ ❖

Learning your words gives wisdom and understanding for
the foolish.   Psalm 119:130

❖ ❖ ❖ ❖ ❖ ❖ ❖ ❖ ❖ ❖ ❖ ❖ ❖ ❖ ❖ ❖ ❖ ❖ ❖

Listen carefully to wisdom; set your mind on understanding.
Then you will understand respect for the LORD, and you will
find that you know God.   Proverbs 2:2, 5

Be patient toward all that is unsolved in your heart.

DAG HAMMARSKJÖLD

 A Life of Faith

Faith means being sure of the things we hope for and
knowing that something is real even if we do not see it.

HEBREWS 11:1

A Solid Foundation

We have this hope as an anchor for the soul,
sure and strong.

Hebrews 6:19

There are not many things in life that can be considered totally secure and immovable. The ground is usually one of them. And yet, all it takes is a shifting fault line to remind you that even the solid foundation beneath your feet is not fully trustworthy.

God has no fault lines. His promises, power, truth, and love are your only true security. When the world around you starts to shake, relationships shift, your health crumbles, or your finances threaten to fall off the deep end, remind yourself of whom you're standing on for support. Rest the full weight of your troubles on the all-powerful God. He's a foundation that will never fail.

In God's faithfulness lies eternal security.
Corrie Ten Boom

Heavenly Father,
It's so comforting to know that You're a solid foundation,
that You are completely secure and trustworthy. Thank You
that when I build my life on You and Your promises, I know
that I'll stand firm, even when trouble comes. With Your help
and guidance, nothing can shake me.

Amen.

Living God's Way

The Highest Standard

All Scripture is inspired by God and is useful for
teaching, for showing people what is wrong in their lives,
for correcting faults, and for teaching how to live right.

2 Timothy 3:16

When you come face-to-face with a dilemma—you had a disagreement with a coworker or the media confronts you with a new worldview—you need to know what's right and wrong, what's acceptable and what is not. You need an authoritative standard by which to measure the issues of life.

The Bible is the ultimate Word on what God has determined is truth or error, morally right or wrong. Just as the National Bureau of Standards in Washington, D.C., sets the mark for weights, measurement, time, and mass, so you have a spiritual Bureau of Standards and Measurements—the Bible.

Everything that comes into your life must be placed alongside the Scriptures to see how it measures up.

The Bible is God's chart for you to steer by, to keep you from the bottom of the sea, and to show you where the harbor is, and how to reach it without running on rocks and bars.

Henry Ward Beecher

Heavenly Father,
Thank You that I do not have to wonder about Your will on any matter: You have given me Your Word to help judge situations both in the world and in my own life. Help me to always use the Bible, the Highest Standard, as my measurement in every circumstance.

Amen.

Taking Action on What You Believe

My brothers and sisters, if people say they have faith,
but do nothing, their faith is worth nothing.

James 2:14

Faith is trust that's put to the test. It acts on what it believes to be true. If you have faith that your best friend can keep a secret, you'll risk being honest about your biggest mistakes and regrets. If you have faith that God really loves you, you'll risk making a decision you believe will honor Him, even if it promises not to be easy.

Faith grows the more you use it, the more you try it on for size. Give God the chance to grow yours. Act on what He's asked you to do. Risk moving out of your comfort level. Do more than believe with your heart. Move forward in faith, wherever He's leading you to go.

Faith is an activity;
it is something that has to be applied.
Corrie Ten Boom

Heavenly Father,
I want to live a life that is characterized by a vibrant, growing faith. I want my faith to be put into action. Help me to take risks that are based on my faith, and cause the faith I have to grow more and more as I trust in You.

Amen.

Can a woman forget
the baby she nurses?
Can she feel no kindness
for the child to
which she gave birth?
Even if she could
forget her children,
I will not forget you.

Isaiah 49:15

*O*ur Changeless God

Our moods may shift, but God's doesn't.

Our minds may change, but God's doesn't.

Our devotion may falter, but God's never does.
Even if we are faithless, He is faithful,
for He cannot betray himself. He is a sure God.

MAX LUCADO

Standing in Belief

Jesus said to Thomas, "Reach your finger here, and look at My hands; and reach your hand here, and put it into My side. Do not be unbelieving, but believing."

John 20:27 NKJV

B elief is not the absence of doubt, but the decision to stand in the midst of your doubts. Thomas had his doubts when the other disciples told him that Jesus had risen from the dead. But when Jesus appeared, He gave him evidence. He simply encouraged Thomas to touch Him and believe.

God doesn't condemn you for your doubts either. He just wants you to reach out to Him, to let Him prove to you that He does indeed exist. He desires to win you with His love and draw you to Him with His kindness. Bring your doubts to Jesus; lay them at His feet in prayer. Let Him turn your doubts to belief.

God has never turned away the
questions of a sincere searcher.
Max Lucado

Heavenly Father,
I know that on this side of heaven not all of my doubts will be resolved. But I choose to stand in faith despite those doubts; I choose to take You at Your Word. Lord, I believe; help my unbelief. I cast my doubts at Your feet and ask You to give me the faith I need to really believe.

Amen.

Change Your Mind

Meditating on God—His character, His miracles, and His
words as communicated in the Bible—helps you understand
more about what God is really like. It helps change your
thinking and even your behavior, from the inside out.

Set aside five uninterrupted minutes today to meditate on
God. Choose one quality of God's character and think about
the difference it makes in your life. Let it lead you to thanks,
to praise, and closer to the heart of God Himself.

ରେ ରେ ରେ ରେ ରେ ରେ ରେ ରେ

*May the words of my mouth and the
meditation of my heart be pleasing in
your sight, O Lᴏʀᴅ, my Rock and my Redeemer.*

Psalm 19:14 ɴɪᴠ

ରେ ରେ ରେ ରେ ରେ ରେ ରେ ରେ

Living God's Way

Oh, taste and see that the LORD is good;
Blessed is the man who trusts in Him.

PSALM 34:8 NKJV

*God is never away off somewhere else.
He is always there.*

Oswald Chambers

154

We know that in everything God works
for the good of those who love him.

ROMANS 8:28

*We do not understand the intricate
pattern of the stars in their courses,
but we know that He who created
them does, and that just as surely as
He guides them, He is charting a safe
course for us.*

Billy Graham

How to Move a Mountain

All things are possible for the one who believes.
Mark 9:23

Have you ever felt your faith in God slipping away? If so, you are not alone. Every life—including yours—is a series of successes and failures, celebrations and disappointments, joys and sorrows. But even when we feel very distant from God, God is never distant from us.

Jesus taught His disciples that if they had faith, they could move mountains. You can too. When you place your faith, your trust, and even your whole life in the hands of Jesus, you'll be amazed at the marvelous things He can do with you and through you. So strengthen your faith through praise, through worship, through Bible study, and through prayer. And trust God's plans. With Him, all things are possible, and

He stands ready to open a world of possibilities for you if you have faith.

Faith in faith is pointless.
Faith in a living, active God moves mountains.
Beth Moore

Heavenly Father,
Even though I'm feeling far from You, I choose to believe that You will get me through every season of faith. Lord, I just ask You to strengthen my faith in You and give me patience and peace.

Amen.

A PRAYER OF FAITH

❖ ❖ ❖ ❖ ❖ ❖ ❖ ❖ ❖ ❖ ❖ ❖ ❖ ❖ ❖

Heavenly Father,

Sometimes the world around me is a fearful place.
Sometimes I get confused, lost amid decisions and deadlines.

In times like these, Father, I pray for Your presence. When
the challenges are overwhelming, give me faith. When I am
filled with doubt, give me faith. And in the joyous moments
of life, keep me mindful that every gift comes from You. In
every aspect of my life, Lord, and in every circumstance,
sustain and build my faith in You.

Amen.

PROMISES FROM GOD'S WORD

Without faith no one can please God. Anyone who comes to
God must believe that he is real and that he rewards those
who truly want to find him.

Hebrews 11:6

❖ ❖ ❖ ❖ ❖ ❖ ❖ ❖ ❖ ❖ ❖ ❖ ❖ ❖ ❖ ❖ ❖ ❖

So faith comes from hearing, that is,
hearing the Good News about Christ.

Romans 10:17 NLT

❖ ❖ ❖ ❖ ❖ ❖ ❖ ❖ ❖ ❖ ❖ ❖ ❖ ❖ ❖ ❖ ❖ ❖

He will keep his agreement forever;
he will keep his promises always.

Psalm 105:8

❖ ❖ ❖ ❖ ❖ ❖ ❖ ❖ ❖ ❖ ❖ ❖ ❖ ❖ ❖ ❖ ❖ ❖

The LORD will protect you from all dangers;
he will guard your life. The LORD will guard you as
you come and go, both now and forever.

Psalm 121:7–8

Living God's Way

ACKNOWLEDGEMENTS:

Elliot, Elisabeth. *Keep a Quiet Heart*
(Ann Arbor: Servant Publications, 1995).

Lea, Larry. *Wisdom: The Gift Worth Seeking*
(Nashville: Thomas Nelson, 1990).

Lotz, Anne Graham. *God's Story*
(Nashville: W Publishing Group, 1999).

Lucado, Max. *Traveling Light*
(Nashville: W Publishing Group, 2000).

Marshall, Catherine. *Moments That Matter*
(Nashville: J Countryman, 2001).

Miller, Paul E. *Love Walked Among Us*
(Colorado Springs: Navpress, 2001).

Wallace, Peter. *What the Psalmist is Saying to You*
(Nashville: Thomas Nelson, 1995).

Warren, Neil Clark. *God Said It, Don't Sweat It*
(Nashville: Thomas Nelson, 1998).